Contents

ABOUT THIS CONTENT 3
WHAT IS INSTRUCTIONAL DESIGN (ID)? 3
    What is an Online Course? 3
    What are the Advantages of Online Training? 5
    What are the Disadvantages of Online Training? 7
GETTING STARTED 9
DECIDING TO WIN! 9
    Pre-Work to Deciding on your Topic 9
    Knowing WHY you are Creating the Training 10
    Determining what makes you UNIQUE 11
ANALYZING COURSE TOPICS 12
    Knowing your Audience 12
    Deciding on the Methodology to be Deployed 13
    Determining the Best Type of Training 21
TESTING YOUR IDEA 28
    Creating a Training Project Plan 28
    Asking your Friends and Family for Opinions 32
    Performing a Need Analysis 32
OUTLINING THE CONTENT 33
    Setting Course Goals and Objectives 33
    Gathering High-Level Content for your Outline 34
    Formalizing the Outline in a Hierarchy 34
    Determining the Type of Menu Structure 36
STORYBOARDING FOR SEQUENCING 37
    Gathering Detailed Content Start to Finish 37
    Creating the Finished Structure for the Storyboard 37
    Storyboard Example 42

Setting the Course of Design 43
Non-Software Tools for Course Creation 43
CREATING YOUR COURSE DESIGN **44**
Designing the Interface 44
Recording and Editing Audio 49
Writing all Printable Job Aids and Materials 50
SCORRING QUIZZES AND LMS LAYOUT **50**
Packaging it all Together and Deploying 50
Setting Reachable Achievements 50
Viewing Analytics and Reports 51
PRICING YOUR COURSE **51**
Running Tempting Discounts 51
Offering Payment Plans and Options 52
Offering a Satisfaction Guarantee 52
MARKETING YOUR OFFERING **52**
Creating a Marketing Plan 52
Creating Non-Electronic Advertising 53
Creating Electronic Advertising 57
LAUNCHING YOUR RESULT **68**
Hosting an Open House 68
Having a Course Kick-Off Party 69
ABOUT H&T DESIGN MEDIA **70**
ABOUT BEVERLY REYNOLDS **70**
AMAZON BOOKS **70**
ONLINE TRAINING COURSES **71**
FREE STUFF **71**

ABOUT THIS CONTENT

You will see sections with a two-column format throughout this content.

These sections provide an overview on the left side of the screen in a bulleted, italicized format and the detailed, paragraph-style to the right.

- *Summary bullets*

    This area will include a detailed description for the bulleted text on the left. It will also include explanations in long-form, examples to illustrate and meanings for all acronyms.

WHAT IS INSTRUCTIONAL DESIGN (ID)?

Instructional Design refers to the writing, designing and developing of courses. Instructional Design often encompasses synonyms or acronyms that can be hard to understand. So, we have included some of the keywords or phrases here:

- *Instructional Systems Design (ISD)*
- *Computer-Based Training (CBT)*
- *Web-Based Training (WBT)*
- *Online Training (OT)*
- *Job Aid (JA)*
- *Step-by-Step (SBS)*
- *Electronic Learning (e-Learning)*
- *On-the-Job Training (OJT)*

What is an Online Course?

- *A sequential grouping of lessons*

    An online course is a grouping of lessons or modules organized in sequential order and packaged together based on a learning path.

A learning path can be based on a position, level or other qualifier.

In other words, the content provided follows a progression conducive to learning on the learner's time frame based on the outcome or objectives set forth by the trainer or training team.

- *Can be role-based*

    Nearly every large corporation has an online university by which specific roles, titles or positions in the organization can be assigned. The university back-end is 'backed' by what is called a Learning Management System (LMS).

- *Enables student progress to be tracked*

    The LMS houses courses, keeps track of student progress and even provides analytics into the overall scoring of the course content, incremental quizzes, and even, a final exam. A comprehensive LMS will provide analytics and reports. We will visit LMS reporting in the "Scoring Quizzes and LMS Tracking" section.

- *Students, user and learners*

    Sometimes you will hear the words 'user,' 'learner' or 'student' used interchangeably throughout this content. These words typically are used synonymously or in place of the other.

- *Acronyms are unavoidable*

    Finally, we will not be quizzing you on the acronyms throughout this course, it is simply to make you more familiar with industry terms and phrases.

You might see these acronyms on a job application site or ad. So, it is a good idea to familiarize yourself with these terms.

What are the Advantages of Online Training?

Online training has several advantages over other types of training that could be implemented, for example:

- Availability – Always Available
- Ability to Refer to the Content
- No Physical Classroom Space Needed
- Ability to Reach Endless Students

Availability – Always Available

- *No need to set hours* — Online training is typically administered via the internet. It can be taken or completed based on the users' schedule. You are not dependent upon set hours of availability.

- *Great for remote users* — This could also be the case if the training is delivered across a company intranet, depending on the setup of the firewall and accessibility for remote users.

Ability to Refer to the Content

- *Retake & Refer* — When training is web-based, unless student access is limited to a specific time, students can refer to the content. This means they can retake the material, refer to their notes and read through as a refresher, if needed.

No Physical Classroom Space Needed

- *Cost-Savings* Sometimes classroom space comes with a rental cost to the trainer, team, organization or company. If you are training 100% online, then the student can train using their current location. This results in a cost-savings in terms of rent, supplies, printouts and food. This also results in a time-savings in terms of paperwork and organizing the rental agreement with an additional 3rd party.

- *Comforts of home* Parents taking the training could train at a home office after the kids are in bed or in an external space, such as the local coffee shop or restaurant.

Ability to Reach Endless Students

- *Unlimited headcount* If you have a classroom of students, you are limited based on the capacity of the room or conference center. However, if you have an online training course, the headcount that can be trained on your course content is limitless.

  Said differently, if the training was written in the language of a user, they can complete your training anywhere.

- *Availability on any device* Users can take the course from their smartphone, iPad, laptop, desktop or any other device that can reach the internet. Nearly any and every device can reach the internet these days, even certain cameras.

- *Time-savings*

    Imagine for a moment that you hold 10 classes to offer a world-wide population. If each of these 10 classes have a total student enrollment of 5,000 unique students, then you have 50,000 total students that your materials have taught within a short amount of time.

    Now think about this, if you took 50,000 students and divided them into classroom trainings in a room that held 40 students at a time, then you would have to comparatively teach each 125 times.
    At the rate of 10 classes multiplied by 125, you would have to teach 1,250 total classroom trainings. That is a very dramatic comparison at a huge time savings.

    In online training, you create the content or training one time, and then you are done creating. Future updates will be needed, but the creation process is complete. Job aids help in the follow up of past students.

What are the Disadvantages of Online Training?

Online training has several disadvantages compared to other types of training that could be implemented, for example:

- *Ability to Gauge Application of Concepts*
- *Settling Peoples' Perception*
- *Accounting for each Learning Style*

Ability to Gauge Application of Concepts

- *Inability to see reactions* — When you are in front of students face-to-face, it is easier to gauge response. You can ask questions to see if they are understanding the material being taught.

- *Cannot guarantee real-life application* — You may never meet one or any of the students enrolled in your training. Therefore, it can be a challenge to see expressions, if they are grasping or taking in what you are saying and if they can truly apply what they learned in real life.

Settling Peoples' Perception

- *Need to show benefits of remote training to some* — Some people still have a negative impression of online training. They may believe that training cannot happen if you are not in physical proximity to the instructor. These individuals that may or may not have embraced this new technology and may require tangible proof of the long-term benefits.

Accounting for each Learning Style

- *Every person learns differently* — Every single person on the face of the planet learns differently than the next person. Some people are visual learners, others learn by listening to audio and others learn through the implementation of both audio and visual cues.

- *Including diagrams as visuals* — Diagrams, graphs, charts and images can be used to illustrate main points and help visual learners remember what they read or heard about in the audio tracks.

- *Anagrams for memory* — An anagram is when we rearrange the letters into something that we can better remember than the word itself. Anagrams go back to the time of the Greeks, so we have them to thank for this type of word association.

GETTING STARTED

There are 10 main steps or areas of implementation when it comes to creating a course within the realm of instructional design. These areas are as follows:

1. Deciding to WIN!
2. Analyzing Course Topics
3. Testing your Idea
4. Outlining the Content
5. Storyboarding for Sequencing
6. Creating the Course Design
7. Scoring Quizzes and LMS Tracking
8. Pricing your Course
9. Marketing your Offering
10. Launching your Result

DECIDING TO WIN!

Pre-Work to Deciding on your Topic

- *Corporate consumption or as entrepreneur?* — When you sit down and dream about creating your first online course, you must first think about whether you are creating a course for corporate consumption or for your own business.

- *Plan for software needs*

    If you are working on your own business, then you will need to plan for software packages and possible training on the functionality before you even think about what topic you want to train your audience.

- *Do you need software training?*

    This course will focus more on the steps needed to be successful from start to finish, but it is agnostic of software names. That is, it is not meant to teach you how to use a specific software package, although we do make specific recommendations throughout the process.

    The final software packages and options you use to create your content is either up to you or the company to which you are employed.

- *Improve user experience as your goal*

    This content will assist you in making choices along the way to improve the user experience based on your knowledge and research.

Knowing WHY you are Creating the Training

- *Know your reason*

    If you are working for a corporation, then they have already mandated why the training must be created. However, if you are creating a course entirely on your own or for your business, then it will be crucial to have in mind the reason you are creating your training.

Real Life Application...

When I created my first online course for my own business after over 20 years of corporate experience, I had a very specific group of reasons I wanted to be an independent online trainer. First, I wanted to stay home with my little boy as much as possible, especially during the summer months.

Second, I had a desire to quit working for someone else and start making a living for myself. I knew that if I could work for myself, then I would gain freedom and flexibility.

I knew at a younger age that I wanted to work as an entrepreneur, even though I was aware of the challenges such as long hours, especially at first. Deciding to work for myself meant a lack of security, but the ability to make my own schedule, choose my insurance and vacation when I wanted.

Finally, I wanted to use the knowledge I already had to help others, regardless of industry. I had participated in all levels of training, design and development. That is, I had 'worn the hat' of technical writer, graphical designer, instructional designer, content developer, and probably most importantly, project manager.

So, as a part of my final 'why' I wanted to take my knowledge and manage a team based on what I had learned so they could enjoy the same freedom and excitement for helping others.

Determining what makes you UNIQUE

- *Know why you believe in you* — You have a unique selling opportunity that no other business around you can boast. That is, there is something, and in fact probably multiple somethings, that set you apart from the rest. These are the reasons that made you believe in you from the very beginning.

- *Realize your value*

  Your job is to realize your value. The unique value you bring above the competition will allow you to be more successful.
  You will find out later that pricing the individual offer should always be based on the unique value that only you can bring to a prospect.

- *Make customers want to repeat with you*

  You want to bring the 'thing' that turns your prospects into customers and your customers into repeat, life-long customers. Your service and your work together should leave them boasting about you around the globe. Keep in mind that word of mouth is far more powerful than we think – both good and bad. Make sure your interactions are far more good than bad. You will not make everyone happy all the time.

ANALYZING COURSE TOPICS

Knowing your Audience

- *Why do they need YOUR solution?*

  When you are a course designer wanting to become a world-class designer, there are two initial questions to answer. The first question to ask yourself is to know why you are creating the training. That is, you have to know the problem you are trying to solve. Second, you need to know for whom the training will exist.

  The design, format and structure of your training will be based on who or the persona that you are training.

- *Create a persona*

    Picture the perfect person to take your training. What do they look like? I DO NOT mean literally, but instead, I want you to think in terms of the role they will play.

    The person could be a stick figure drawing, but you need to know the qualities, profession and habits of your average learner.

- *Design elements to match the persona*

    For example, if you are creating training for a teenage crowd, you are likely to use a striking, edgy design of bright hues.

    Whereas, if you are dealing with an older crowd and creating training on the latest updates to the AARP system updates, you will likely use the simplest path, go for ease of navigation and use larger, less-edgy fonts.

Deciding on the Methodology to be Deployed

There are several training methodologies that can be deployed. We will discuss the most popular methodologies at the time of this content.

ADDIE

NOTE: *This content was taken from and adapted from "Getting the Life of an Instructional Designer" by Beverly A. Reynolds; published in 2017; ISBN# 9781546429050.*

ADDIE is a popular training methodology or delivery model. As you might have suspected, ADDIE stands for the following as an acronym:

- *Analyze*
- *Design*
- *Develop*
- *Implement*
- *Evaluate*

- *Analyze viability based on need* — This methodology states that a training team or training team member starts by analyzing a project and the viability based on need. He or she compares the project objectives to the objectives of the company or organization.

- *Assuming the organization goals are in alignment, the content is outlined* — If they are in alignment, then they move to creating an outline with actionable items. Next, they turn the action items into a detailed storyboard. This section gives you an idea of what the product *might* look like at the time of completion. The work is then carried out, the project is implemented and user feedback is continually sought after the implementation date.

Monetizing E-Learning Courseware

Let's look at a breakdown of each of the parts of this acronym from Analyze to Evaluate:

Phase	Overview	Output / Event
ANALYZE	The thought is that you start by looking at the business need, developing objectives and determining a roadmap for project completion on-time and within budget.	Business Analysis, Project Plan, Goals and Objectives
DESIGN	An instructional designer or technical writer authors the content, regardless of delivery method, in an outline translated to a storyboard template.	Outline, Storyboard, Wireframe, Quiz Questions
DEVELOP	One or more developers create the navigation, interactions, instructional content and provide positive/negative pathing to give the average user choices to support their learning style.	Interface, Quiz Interactions, Printable Job Aids
IMPLEMENT	Upon successful completion of the timeline and objectives, it is important to deploy the final training solution or final product.	Go-Live Date / Event, Marketing, Solution Deployment

Phase	Overview	Output / Event
EVALUATE	After you have deployed your training, it is important to monitor feedback, make changes to the content or interactions and stay involved with your students or stakeholders.	Learning Survey, User Follow-Up, Repeat Business Achieved, Stakeholder Communication

Now we will take a more detailed approach...

ANALYZE:

- *Analyze the business and know what your course will solve*
  The first step of this phase is to analyze the business problem at hand. You need to know what your training course will solve. This can be done with a training project plan complete with deadlines, goals and objectives. This will provide a roadmap for the entire life of the project from start to finish.

- *Take the timeline and set the scope*
  Second, would be to take the timeline and set the scope. The scope of the project will help you think about the main sections of the outline. We will visit the outline in greater detail later, but the outline helps you put order to the content at a high-level - making the storyboard process easier as well.

DESIGN:

- *Use of a storyboard template*

    Now, an instructional designer or technical writer will author the content of the training, regardless of delivery method, in an outline translated into a storyboard template.

- *Add structure and imagery*

    The whole purpose of the storyboard is to help you put structure and imagery to the text. The visuals used will help to 'paint a picture' for the audience.

DEVELOP:

- *Implement interactions, navigation and pathing*

    This is the phase in which one or more developers create the navigation, interactions, instructional content and provide positive and negative navigation pathing to give the average user choices.

- *Next/Previous versus skip around*

    For example, if the user wants to navigate a computer-based course using the Next button AND could skip around or back through topics for increased understanding with the use of a menu structure.

IMPLEMENT:

- *Deploy the total solution*

    Upon successful completion of the timeline and training objectives it is important to deploy the final training solution or final product.

EVALUATE:

- *Monitor feedback ad make changes* — After you have deployed your training, it is important to monitor feedback, make changes to the content or interactions and stay involved through communication with your students or stakeholders. This will be especially important if you are monetizing.

- *Track progress through reporting and stay in contact with students* — If your course is run through a Learning Management System or LMS, you can track progress through reporting. An LMS makes it possible to see how many students have started your course compared to the total enrollment, how many have completed the training, and oftentimes, how they scored on either incremental or final quizzes (if scored).

As a final piece of this section, let me provide you with a course checklist as it pertains to the ADDIE model.

Check	Checklist Item
ANALYZE	
Determine the business problem	
Write the course overview and summary text	
Provide the project vision statement based on the company or client vision statement	
Author the main course goal	
Add in the actionable objectives	
Construct a basic outline	
DESIGN	
Check for content completion in the finished outline	
Construct a full storyboard	

Check	Checklist Item
Determine the graphics to be used	
Check for consistencies in the context and overall flow	
Site all references	
Audit your navigation mentioned in storyboard	
Know your audience – have a test audience	
Create your own style guide if one does not already exist	
Vary the types of training offered	
DEVELOP	
Create the design of the interface	
Ensure there are multiple paths, if applicable (e.g., Next/Previous, menus)	
Verify interactions	
Create the buttons and states for each	
Ensure all images have a caption or figure number	
Page numbering is present	
Progress can be viewed by user	
User can pause the audio, if necessary or requested	
Audio files are linked and edited	
The visual presentation is eye-pleasing	
Colors are consistent	
Branding is in place and noticeable	
Logo placement is consistent	
Audio can be turned on and off, if requested	
Corporate standards are adhered	
Every page has a title and sub-titles, as necessary and appropriate	
The client has viewed incremental demos of the end product along the timeline	
All links are well-tested	

Check	Checklist Item
Develop a feedback mechanism	
Quizzes are scored and weighted	
IMPLEMENT	
Kickoff is held with food and invites	
Course is bookmarked and ready for publishing	
Final testing is a success	
EVALUATE	
Users are providing feedback	
Incorporate on-going feedback	

Scrum

NOTE: *This content was taken from and adapted from "Getting the Life of an Instructional Designer" by Beverly A. Reynolds; published in 2017; ISBN# 9781546429050.*

- *A framework for rapid project completion*
  Scrum is a framework for creating and maintaining a consistent rate of work for complex projects, programs and portfolios based on ever-changing needs of the stakeholders or business.

- *Smaller team size*
  Scrum teams are typically small in size. If a scrum team has more than 3 to 9 members, it is typically broken into additional scrum teams so the work can be completed in the most efficient method. Smaller teams can knowledge-share more easily than larger teams.

- *An Agile methodology (incremental development framework)*
  Scrum is still the most popular of the Agile methodologies. That is, it is NOT the only Agile methodology for training or development.

- *What is a project?* — A project is a collaborative effort to produce a feature, product or service based on a vision statement and value to the customer. Scrum focuses on the delivery of a project in iterative cycles or sprints – no matter the type of project.

Scrum has six main principles for which every project is to be built:

- Empirical Process Control
- Self-Organization
- Collaboration
- Value-Based Prioritization
- Time-Boxing
- Iterative Development

- *Each methodology requires time-management* — No matter the training methodology to be deployed, you are generally bound to the timeline and confines of the approver, client or customer. Now, let's look at the different training types available.

Determining the Best Type of Training

- *Training delivery can be online or in-person* — There are many, many types of ways that training can be delivered. Some of these options are electronic-based, such as online training. Other types of training can be delivered through in-person or classroom delivery.

  The next few headings detail several of the most popular training delivery types.

Classroom Presentation / Teleconference materials

- *Handouts help set expectations* — If you are hosting a classroom training session, you will likely need to not only prepare the PowerPoint-type presentation, but possibly also classroom supplies, expectations and printed handouts.

Bound Chapter Book or e-Book

Regardless of whether you are authoring a printed hardcover or softcover book or supplying readers with an electronic e-Book version, you will need to do the following:

- Write in the proper language
- Format your book chapters with headings, sub-heads, sections and page numbering
- Design the layout and the cover
- Write your author biography
- Choose and add all graphics, pull quotes and any visual elements
- Write the book back content and spine
- Market your book through specific channels or go with a publisher
- Depending on the publishing option and output type selected, you may also have to purchase an ISBN #

Graphics, Logos, Icons, Buttons (all states) and Combination Marks

- *Images aid in the training experience* — Sometimes images can be used to help train or aid in the training experience. That is, graphics can 'tell a story.' A logo identifies who published the training.

Monetizing E-Learning Courseware

A combination mark is like a logo, but it contains an image and text.

- *Buttons have an up, down and over state*

    Now let's visit buttons. Nearly every course contains buttons. Oftentimes these buttons consist of three different states: Up, Down and Over.

    That is, the button itself will look different before the user clicked it, after the user clicked it and while the mouse is hovered over the image.

Software Simulations

- *Simulations emulate a software or processes*

    Simulations are movies created with a specific type of software that allows you to emulate the functionality of a process or software application. These movies allow the user to feel as if they are in the actual software without fear of 'messing something up' since they are using a practice environment.

- *Several software packages can be used*

    There are several pieces of software such as Adobe® Captivate™, that enable a training developer to create an environment that is similar to what the user will experience. For instance, if the user needs to learn how to use Microsoft Excel, a training developer could create a simulation that allows the user to practice functions or pivot tables.

- *Shows you how a process works*

    Simulations show the user how a piece of software or functionality works by having the mouse pointer navigate without the user having to use the mouse to navigate.

- *Let's you try the process or functionality* — There is a second type of simulation that allows the user to try the functionality in what feels like a practice environment before they actually go to the actual software or process.

- *Allows you to be evaluated* — The third type of simulation is one which evaluates the user either on a set of steps or based on questions that the user answers along the way.

Real Life Application…..

I remember when I first earned my very first job as an instructional designer. I remember being very nervous due to a lack of experience. My new co-workers treating me as a true professional, even though I had never been involved in this line of work.

I remember that everything from the types of training, methodologies and software I would be using were all brand new. I quickly learned that there were three different types of simulations. These types included the following:

- Show Me
- Let Me Try OR Try Me
- Evaluate Me

Now, almost 20 years later, those phrases still stick in my mind and I think of them in my own business. Those same phrases can be applied to all kinds of areas in life outside of software simulations.

For instance, in the books I write I need to make sure I tell users about the subject. Then, I need to give them more detail, and after that, try to have some sort of interactivity, quiz or homework.

Corporate Communications

- *Some corporate communications are outsourced*

  Some companies offer corporate communications to their staff. These are often electronic bulletins sent via email with paper copies distributed in key areas of the building.
  These bulletins may be written in-house, by the training team or outsourced to third-party companies or vendors.

- *These communications educate on new policies and more*

  Such bulletins can be used to educate people on new building practices, new employee rules, a new handbook and more. The list of ways this document type can be used is seemingly endless.

E-Mail Templates

Email can be an effective means of communication that can be used in so many ways:

- An email campaign to tell your e-mail list or corporation that a course is about to go-live
- As a way to obtain pre-sales for your offerings

NOTE: You can use the e-mail signature that gets placed at the bottom of every email as a means of advertising your courses.

Overview Job Aids

- *Can be printable, electronic or both*

  A job aid provides a summary of the business process or functionality. It is usually presented in a printable and electronic format.

A job aid enables you to read about a subject and have a better understanding of the history, rationale or current state.

- *Can be role-based*
  This type of targeted documentation might be created for a set of roles, industry or region. In other words, nearly all types of people could benefit if the training is tailored to their specific needs.

- *May include charts or visuals*
  It may include a flowchart created in a diagraming software, such as Microsoft® Visio™ or Microsoft® Excel™. Sometimes these diagrams have symbols or swim lanes.

- *Can be created for any audience*
  The benefits of this type of training can be almost endless since they are versatile and can be consumed by any type of individual at any time or place.

- *Could be a Glossary, Q&A, etc.*
  A fantastic example of a job aid document might be a glossary of terms, Q&A document or a series of charts.

Step-by-Step Materials

- *Provides steps to completion*
  Much like a typical job aid, a step-by-step document is often available in an electronic and printable format within nearly any organization.

  However, instead of simply providing an overview of a process or functionality, the step-by-step file is literally a 'How To' document for a specific set of instructions.

Computer-Based (CBT) / Web-Based Training (WBT)

- *Considered interactive training*

  This type of training is considered interactive training. It is delivered to the audience as a computer-based or web-based training. I know what you are thinking, aren't they the same thing? My answer is that today they are used synonymously.

- *CBT / WBT has many navigational components*

  A CBT / WBT might have a complex menu system, breadcrumbs, button interactions, alternative or pathed navigation, intro text, summary text, graphics, animations and an eye-catching layout and design.

Complex, Branched Help Systems

- *Help systems link topic-to-topic*

  Perhaps you are writing a complex help system that branches out based on clickable hyperlinks. Oftentimes, help systems are accessible by clicking <F1> on the keyboard while logged into a specific software package.

- *Can be configurable*

  Help systems can be configured in a multitude of different ways, much like training courses, but they are most often a series of 'How To' topics that help a user know how to navigate from screen-to-screen or tell them how to complete one or more procedures or functions.

Real Life Application…..

Several years ago, I was employed by a larger hospitality company that used a large, branching help system created in Adobe® RoboHelp™. This application allowed us to create customized training based on role and it would link parts of the application to 'How To' topics specific to that aspect or piece of functionality.

We also made the topics region-specific. Therefore, if you were from a different state or country and had different rules or regulations, you could click to find details specific to your processes.

It was the job of the training team to author all the topics and ensure they were properly linked with the correct security and login details.

TESTING YOUR IDEA

Creating a Training Project Plan

- *A training plan will avoid pitfalls along the way*
  It is essential to have a training plan in place before you embark on your course creation adventure. That is, you should formalize the efforts that will be needed in terms of tasks, timeline, dependencies, resources, and even, your approvers.

- *Project plans are never 'set in stone' and should be changeable*
  The following image provides a good guide in terms of the columns that your project plan should include. That does not mean that you couldn't add more details, but keep in mind that this is a document that will help you as a guide throughout the project lifecycle.

Monetizing E-Learning Courseware

- *Choose the appropriate software* — The training project plan could be completed in any software, such as Microsoft® Project™ (great for visual representation of the 'big picture') or Microsoft® Excel™.

The following diagram provides a good basis for you to begin to organize the groundwork needed for your courseware. Keep in mind that the columns have been modified to fit within the pages of this book, but your view or orientation might be landscape instead of portrait.

Task	% Complete	Total Duration	Start	End	Dependencies	Predecessors	Resource Type	Resource Initials	Approver Initials
Create Outline	25	1W	6/1/18	6/7/18	Needs Analysis	Needs Analysis	IH	BR	ID
Create Course Design	0	2W	6/9/18	6/23/18	Outline Complete	Outline Complete	3P	?	BR

Let's breakdown the columns from the previous image:

TASK:

The task is the individual assignment that may or may not have to be completed before another task or assignment can begin.

29 | Page

% COMPLETE:

The percent complete should show a numerical value. This number is typically represented without the percent sign and most often as one of the following:

- Increments of 10
- Increments of 25
- >= 0
- <= 100

TOTAL DURATION:

The detail in this column is most often a numerical value followed by one of the following letters:

- D for Days
- W for Weeks
- M for Months
- Y for Years

START:

This is the start date of the current row or task and should be reflected as XX/XX/XX or XX/XX/XXXX (each X represents a single numerical value or 0).

END:

This is the end date of the current row or task and should be reflected as XX/XX/XX or XX/XX/XXXX (each X represents a single numerical value or 0).

DEPENDENCIES:

This could list the tasks by name or link back to the sheet cells that correspond to the tasks that must be completed prior to the start of the current task or row.

Monetizing E-Learning Courseware

PREDECESSORS:

This could list the tasks by name or link to the sheet cells that correspond to the tasks that must be at least started prior to the start of the current task/row.

RESOURCE TYPE:

The detail in this column typically shows as one of the following:

- IH for In-House
- IT for Intra-Team
- ET for External Team
- 3P for Third-Party

NOTE: *Keep in mind that if you type ET or 3P, since these resources are outside of you or your team, you may need to build in the time it takes to communicate back and forth into your milestones and timeline.*

RESOURCE INITIALS:

This is the name or initials of the person(s) <u>responsible for the work</u> on this task. This could be an in-house/intra-team, inter-team or 3rd party name or team.

NOTE: *Notice in the previous diagram that we added a question mark. It is totally acceptable to have question marks in rows or columns at the start of the project, but this should be a document that is updated throughout the project.*

APPROVER INITIALS:

This is the name or initials of the persons <u>responsible for the approval</u> of this task. This could be an in-house/intra-team, inter-team or 3rd party name.

Asking your Friends and Family for Opinions

- *Poll the right people regarding new ideas*

    When asking your friends and family for advisement on your course topic or name, be careful to ask the right people.

    When I say, "right people" I am not necessarily talking about the people that always agree with you but those that will give you honest feedback and maybe even make intelligible suggestions that will positively impact your business and decisions.

Performing a Need Analysis

- *Determine the problem*

    The Needs Analysis is often called a Needs Assessment. In this step, you determine a problem that needs to be solved by the users or organization, research what is currently being done to solve the issue and find ways for YOU to 'be the answer.'

- *Solve the problem*

    The problem is typically something the target audience or average user struggles to solve on their own. Your training MUST not only solve the issue at hand, but also offer a unique solution or provide a set of recommended future actions.

OUTLINING THE CONTENT

Setting Course Goals and Objectives

- *Goals and objectives are NOT same* — People tend to think of goals and objectives as being interchangeable. However, they are actually quite different from one another.

- *Goals are the focal point of achievement* — The goal of a course is what the course aims to achieve. In other words, the goal tells why the course is being written in the first place.
  If you were to create a course about how to create online courseware, then the goal might look something like this:

  > The goal of this course is to help trainers and business owners better understand the steps of course creation from analyzing the business problem to deploying the solution.

- *Objectives set expectations* — The objectives tell the user what they can expect to learn from successful completion of the training. These items are actionable.

  If you were to stick with the same example, then your objectives might look similar to this:

By the end of the "How to Create and Monetize your Online Training" course, students will be able to:

- *Analyze the business problem so the scope can be set*
- *Author an outline to maximize topic inclusion*
- *Create a storyboard to improve content flow*
- *Create an interactive course that engages*
- *Deploy and gauge student satisfaction*

Gathering High-Level Content for your Outline

- *Brainstorm a few ideas and write down facts* — When it comes to gathering content, it is good to brainstorm a few topics. Start by writing down the facts that you know and the questions that you have to begin filling in the gaps.

- *Write down everything to a clearer picture* — Once you have written down everything you know about the topic, it will become glaringly clearer as to what your main topics are. This will help you come up with the Roman Numerals for the outline.

Formalizing the Outline in a Hierarchy

- *Determine the level of your outline and main sections* — Your outline may follow typical Roman Numeral hierarchy like the table of contents of a book. You can decide how deep the numbering or lettering goes based on the depth and scope of content being covered.

Monetizing E-Learning Courseware

Here is a basic outline example:

How to Create and Monetize your Online Training

I. Analyze the problem to be solved
   a. Decide on the topic
   b. Create training business plan
   c. Write goals and objectives
II. Outline your Content
   a. Set your levels of hierarchy
III. Write the Storyboard
   a. Author the detailed content
   b. Start to think of the imagery
   c. Set the type of training
   d. Write quiz questions
IV. Create the Course Interface
   a. Design the layout of the training
   b. Develop all interactions
   c. Create the printable job aids
   d. Add the finishing touches by testing all content
V. Deploy the Training to the Business
   a. Decide how the content will be packaged
   b. Publish the course
   c. Monitor feedback

- *The amount of content decides how the outline progresses* Your course might be a self-contained course with a menu structure where the users navigate around a single file, or your course might include several, individual movies that are 'strung together.' Either way, the amount of content may very well decide how the outline progresses.

- *The outline aids in the storyboard creation*
  Once your outline is in place, it will be much easier to create the storyboard since you have already put the initial structure and order in place.
  This order MUST remain unchanged throughout the life of the project.

- *Start with the initial problem in mind*
  The final, and probably the most important thing to remember when creating your outline, is that you need to start with the initial problem to be solved and work almost backwards through the steps of the solution.

Determining the Type of Menu Structure

- *Let the LMS guide your structure*
  Your menu structure could take on a multitude of forms based on the format of the training being produced.

  For instance, if you are doing a series of selfie-styled movies, then the LMS will be your menu structure.

- *Menus 'drive' the navigation*
  However, if you will have a stand-alone course that popups up from within the LMS, then your menu could be one of the following options:

    - *A series of drop-down menus accessed by buttons across the top of the course screen*

    - *A left-side menu that pops out from the left and either changes the viewable area or opens over the content*

- *Bookmarking is a great LMS feature* — Each LMS is different in whether it keeps track of user progress by bookmarking or if you need to build in a progress slider to mark the course complete.

STORYBOARDING FOR SEQUENCING

Gathering Detailed Content Start to Finish

- *Start with blank grid pages and a topic per grid/page* — When gathering the details to be added to your storyboard, you might consider printing off several blank pages (one grid per page with blank spaces). Start writing a new topic on each page with as many details and questions as you know for each page topic.

- *Rearrange the grids in sequential order* — Once you have all questions answered on each page, you can arrange each piece of paper in order. This will tell you what pages need to be split out into additional pages to avoid a single page being too text-heavy and to keep the audio brief on each page.

Creating the Finished Structure for the Storyboard

- *A storyboard 'sets the stage' for the length and scope of the training* — The storyboard is a physical means for organizing content. Your storyboard helps you design your material and helps you answer the following questions:

    1.) How much detail is needed per topic? What are the remaining questions?
    2.) How many pages will each topic take up based on the real estate on each page?
    3.) What type of menu will be needed for the scope?

Here is an example of a storyboard that you can apply to your course design:

STORYBOARD TEMPLATE	
Page Title:	
Path/Breadcrumbs:	
Graphics:	**Interaction:**
Content *(for a single page):*	
Audio *(if different than the content):*	
Progression:	
Quiz Questions:	

Page Title:

This section should include the Page Title and tell users what they can expect to read or hear on the current page.

Path/Breadcrumbs:

- *Breadcrumbs allow a quick means to navigate forward and backward*

  The pathway is how the user would return to the current page and allows quick access links to previously-visited pages in the progression.

  For example, if users were taking an HR Policies course and clicked the Policies menu, and then clicked the Sexual Harassment menu option, then the path below the title might read as follows:

Policies > Sexual Harassment

- *Sub-menus must be considered in overall navigation* Given this example, we would assume the user is currently on the Sexual Harassment page. If there had been another layering, such as a sub-menu selection, then the progression might look something like the following:

Policies > <u>Harassment Overview</u> > Sexual Harassment

For users to return to the Harassment overview, you would need to make the text clickable with a link and perhaps be noted with blue or distinct text.

Graphics:

- *Images must support the page contents* This area of your storyboard would show or describe the image to be on the current page. You will want to make sure the image you use supports your text and that it is a royalty-free image or that you have paid to use the image using the right usage-based contract.

- *Some images are FREE and some come with a fee* Oftentimes, when you go to a site, such as Canva.com, some images are free and some come at a fee. If the image comes with a fee, then you must read the agreement. Some images specify how many times it can be printed and/or a digital-usage fee.

Interaction:

- *All images should be approved by the approver*
  If there is going to be an animation, then you will want to list the animation with a description, especially if a third-party or client is approving your storyboard. Your animation may describe how the user will interact with the page.

- *Not every page will need an interaction*
  For instance, your graphics section may make mention of an animated .GIF, animated page transition or it could tell that the user will have a matching or other on-screen exercise. Not every page will have an interaction.

Content:

- *All on-screen text should be planned*
  This is the dedicated area where you will plan the on-screen text that will be visible on the screen. This could simply be bulleted text with the bulk of the content only available in the audio.

- *Consider the audience*
  Keep in mind the type of audience you will be training. Certain audiences will want to see all the screen and be printable, while others will find it acceptable to only show short pieces of text or phrases to simplify the screen design.

Audio:

- *Audio text may differ from on-screen text*
  As mentioned in the Content area, this could be an exact replica of what is in the Content section, or it could be a longer version of what is seen on-screen.

- *Rewind and fast forward?*

  Either way, the content in this section will serve as an audio script if audio will be available for the course.

  You may have taken a course somewhere along your training journey that allows audio to be turned on and off. Some courses allow you to rewind and fast forward. Another grouping of courses does not contain audio at all. For these types of courses, this section would be blank.

Progression:

- *Give the user navigation options*

  This area notes how users will progress to the next page of content. Users could navigate forward and back with Next and Previous buttons. Sometimes the navigation auto-progresses.

- *Doers your course have linked videos?*

  That is, some courses are comprised of videos that automatically play the next video in the sequence, either immediately or after a specified amount of time.

Quiz Questions:

- *Use different question types*

  There are several types of quiz questions you can employ, including:

  1.) Matching
  2.) Long Answer
  3.) Short Answer
  4.) True/False
  5.) Multiple Choice
  6.) Games

Your quizzes could be a scored assessment or a non-scored self-assessment.

Storyboard Example

Here is an example of a storyboard structure using a realistic example from this content:

STORYBOARD EXAMPLE	
Page Title: Deciding to WIN!	
Path/Breadcrumbs: Deciding to WIN! > Pre-Work to Deciding on your Topic	
Graphics: Include a picture of an open book with pages flipping	**Interaction:** Not applicable
Content *(for a single page)*: Pre-Work to Deciding on your Topic • Corporate consumption or as a part of YOUR business • You will need to learn software prior to getting started • Put in the time for proper knowledge and research	
Audio *(if different than the content)*: When you sit down and dream about creating your first online course, you must first think about whether you are creating a course for corporate consumption or for your own business. If you are working on your own business, then you will need to plan for software packages and possible training on the functionality before you even think about what topic you want to train your audience.	

This course will focus more on the steps needed to be successful from start to finish, but it is agnostic of software names.

That is, it is not meant to teach you how to use a specific software package, although we do make specific recommendations throughout the process. The final software packages and options you use to create your content is either up to you or the company to which you are employed.

This training content will assist you in making choices along the way to improve the user experience based on your knowledge and research.

Progression:
Auto-progression, Video content

Quiz Questions:
Not applicable

Setting the Course of Design

Some people are able to have a team of writers, designers and developers. Other people become their own one-stop-shop as an individual business owner.

Either way, if you have a dream, never stop until you have achieved success. Even if that means you have to work long hours, learn complex software and purchase non-software tools.

Non-Software Tools for Course Creation

Just like software, there are several tools that may need to be learned or purchased. Some of these tools include:

NOTE: *These items were standards at the time this content was created and published.*

Non-Software Tools	*Examples*
Microphone	Desk Stand: blue® The Snowball Lapel: Sony®
Sound Proofing	Foam wall panels
Studio Space and Backdrops	Dedicated office space just for this type of work; could be in-house, in-home or rented office space
Lighting Stands and Light Bulbs	Might be formal stands or generic ones purchased from a hardware store; Use daylight bulbs; do not rely solely with outdoor lighting if inside
Camera – Video, Cell	Nikon® SLR, Canon® Rebel™
Camera Memory Cards	MicroSD card, small portable drives
External Hard Drives	Any manufacturer

CREATING YOUR COURSE DESIGN

Designing the Interface

- *Material should flow sequentially*   Now it is time to design the training course interface.

There are several elements of design that MUST be added so users can learn from you and take in your material sequentially. The items listed in this section are just the minimum amount of choices you will have when it comes to training.

- *Ensure consistency* — Not all these items may be needed for every course you design, but it will give you things to think about along the way and help you ensure consistency with each course you create.

Adding a Course Overview

- *Set the scope* — The course overview is important to every course, no matter which style of course you design. This text needs to be a few paragraphs in length and tell the user what is included. In a sense, the overview tells the user they are taking the right course.

- *Capture the attention of your audience* — Overview text should give the users enough information to get them wanting to read more. Keep in mind the vast majority of courses are never finished, even if users are paying for the content. They either get bored, go straight to the quizzes or just lose interest in the topic. So, you MUST capture their attention at the start. This will help users want to purchase more courses from YOU!

Writing the Glossary

- *Provide a list of terms and definitions* — The glossary is a list of terms and definitions. The point of this is to give the user a printable resource as they go through your content. This reference can be referred to over and over again. Additionally, there is a benefit to you as well.

- *Make the Glossary or other files printable* — In fact, when you add a glossary, if you place it as a printable job aid at the beginning of the course, you can instruct your audience to print the resource so you can use the acronyms throughout. Just make sure that you explain the acronym prior to using it continuously.

- *Make files downloadable for future* — Finally, the glossary can be a method of learning past the last date of access for the course or the date of completion.

Having Breadcrumbs

- *Include pathing or alternative navigation* — Breadcrumbs provide pathing or an alternative means of navigation so that users can visit or re-visit specific topics. Breadcrumbs also provide a means of returning to previous or referenced topics. Think of them as 'hotspots' that are clickable in text.

- *Allow users to 'find their way' around your content* — When I think of breadcrumbs, I think of the movie E.T. In this movie, the young boy, Elliott, was searching for E.T. and wanted to find his way home. So, he dropped candy on the pathway in attempts to be able to find his way back.

The breadcrumbs of your course work in much the same idea – providing 'a way back' for your students.

Adding Page Numbering

- *Numbering can differ in printed materials*

  Page numbering can differ between the course content and the printable material. In printed material, page numbering can be the same on the left and right or different than the other. Additionally, the numbering can differ in terms of formatting and style on the first or last page and between the sections too.

- *Test your numbering before publishing*

  In a course, page numbering can start on the first page of content and keep going through to the end of the content or start over again as a new menu option is introduced. Be sure that regardless of the numbering style used, you test both the course and all printed materials for consistency and accuracy.

Incorporating Navigational Buttons

- *The style of the course drives the button types*

  At a minimum, if you have a self-contained course, you will want to have a Home option and a Next and Previous button set. The style of your course drives the types of buttons and if specific button options are present or not.

- *Include button states (e.g., Up, Down, Over)*

  As always, if you use physical buttons, make sure that each button has different states, such as Up, Down and Over.

This will likely take knowledge of software packages such as Adobe® Photoshop™ or some other graphics or vector-based program.

Deploying a Progress Bar

- *Keep your sections short and include a progress indicator* — A progress bar lets the user know how far they have progressed or made it through a single movie or the course. Remember that peoples' attention spans are short nowadays, so it is a good idea to create your sections and your movies less than 10 minutes in length.

- *Break up long content* — If your content becomes longer than that, it is a good idea to break up the content into smaller chunks, such as Part 1 and Part 2 and more, if needed.

Implementing the Logo

- *Add your logo for repetitive recognizability* — Your company or organization logo should be on every single page of your course. If in a selfie-styled movie, it should at least be in an animated intro. The reason for this is repetitive recognizability. Adding your logo to any course or publication should be adding your own name.

Including an On/Off Audio Option

- *Determine if your course will have audio and if the user will have control* — Some courses have the ability for audio to be turned on or off by the user. That is, the course contains buttons that give the user full control of the audio. Sometimes this means that they can only turn the audio on and off, but the volume must be controlled on the workstation.

- *Location matters in terms of audio* — Some courses do not allow audio because students will be taking the courses on open workstations. Other courses allow full control to include volume too. The location at which the user will be taking the course might make a difference in terms of audio.

TIP! *Remember, you always want to set expectations ahead of time so a user knows if they even need to supply headphones or not to complete the course.*

Adding a Course Summary

- *The summary content pulls the entire course together for the user* — Every successful course sums the content together with a summary statement or a grouping of paragraphs that pull all the content together. The summary should confirm the scope of the course and tell the user what they learned as a means of confirmation and affirmation.

Recording and Editing Audio

- *Choose a camera, lighting and background* — When I record my videos, I use a simple video camera, custom lighting and a simple background or solid backdrop. Once I have a clean recording, I import the video to a software called VideoPad® Video Editor™. There are additional choices on the market, but this is my program of choice.

- *Choose your timings wisely* — I love the flexibility, timings and text that I can add to my videos to customize the user experience.

Once my video is edited, I can upload the final product into my course or place the final rendition on social media.

Writing all Printable Job Aids and Materials

- *Job aids can be repurposed* — Job aids and all printed materials can be repurposed into other types of deliverables. In terms of the course, job aids can have a shelf life long after the course access has ended. Be sure to carry through with the same 'look and feel.'

SCORRING QUIZZES AND LMS LAYOUT

Packaging it all Together and Deploying

- *Test all links before deploying* — After you have finished writing, designing and developing your training content, it is important to test all the links of your interface. Additionally, it is crucial that you proof and spellcheck as well.

- *Be prepared for all kinds of feedback from users* — Once all checks have been completed, you must package it up and get it ready for 'primetime.' That is, be ready to have your course deployed and be mentally prepared for both positive and negative feedback from your userbase.

Setting Reachable Achievements

- *Set achievable benchmarks* — When you deploy a course to the marketplace or organization, be sure to create achievable benchmarks. That is, be sure to set goals for each type of analytics you want to be able to run day-to-day, month-over-month and year-over-year.

- *Goals should stretch your idea of what is possible* — These goals should be a stretch to what you currently think is possible. This is oftentimes called a 'stretch goal.' Stretch goals 'stretch' what you think might be conceivably possible.

Viewing Analytics and Reports

- *Track from the go-live date* — You will want to monitor the success of each course from the go-live date for at least the first year in production. This will help you with market trends, user habits and the 'wins' of you and your team.

- *Know what you want to track* — Here are some of the metrics you many want to track:

    1.) Student behavior post-completion
    2.) Course completion rates
    3.) Average course session length
    4.) Most popular lessons or modules
    5.) User survey feedback
    6.) Total length of stay in a given course
    7.) Retention rates and more...

PRICING YOUR COURSE

Running Tempting Discounts

- *There are several advantages to you and your customers* — Here are some of the advantages of running temporary discounts – whether pre-sales or seasonal/situational):

    1.) Help you meet sales goals
    2.) Aid your satisfaction ratings
    3.) Attract customers and clients

Offering Payment Plans and Options

- *Lower payments mean an increase is customers*

  There are several benefits of offering payment plans to your userbase:

  1.) Creates lower payments over time
  2.) Increases customer availability

Offering a Satisfaction Guarantee

- *You do not have to agree to offer a guarantee*

  A satisfaction guarantee allows the user to contact you or your company for their full or partial money back if the student or user feels as though the quality does not meet their satisfaction – for any reason. By offering a guarantee, you are not saying you agree with the student or customer if you give all or a portion of their money back.

- *Help the user feel good about their buying decision*

  Satisfaction guarantees help make the user feel good about their buying decision. Remember that in sales the customer or student is ALWAYS right. This is a key point to remember, even when it is hard.

MARKETING YOUR OFFERING

Creating a Marketing Plan

When you consider marketing your business – you need a marketing plan.

- *Your plan should inspire you and others*

  This plan should inspire those looking for YOUR solution to act by choosing to support your business and be efficient in approach.

Monetizing E-Learning Courseware

That is, you need to carefully plan how you will deal with geography, printed media and advertising, merchandise and materials, printing considerations, color usage, marketing streams and available statistics.

Creating Non-Electronic Advertising

NOTE: *This content was taken from and adapted from "How to Create Enterprise-Level Branding for YOUR Business" by Beverly Reynolds; published in 2018; ASIN #* **B07DL5VS4T.**

Non-Electronic Marketing Streams	Used in PAST	Use TODAY	Want to use in the FUTURE
Word of Mouth Typical, everyday conversation			
Door-to-Door Early registration incentives			
Park Bench Advertisements Plaque or engraving			
[Side of] School Bus Advertisements Caters to specific audiences			
Shopping Cart Advertisements Caters to a			

Non-Electronic Marketing Streams	Used in PAST	Use TODAY	Want to use in the FUTURE
broader audience			
Billboards Appropriately-sized text for viewing from afar			
Call Center Cold Calling Based on a scripted message			
TV Ads or Programming ($$ typically more expensive $$)			
Vendor Booth with a Drawing Festival participation			
Online Contest Reward, scholarship or monetary gift			
Radio Can be streamed			

Monetizing E-Learning Courseware

Non-Electronic Marketing Streams	Used in PAST	Use TODAY	Want to use in the FUTURE
across the internet			
Newspaper (offer to write a story in exchange for ad space)			
Magazine Ads Charged based on characteristics, size of the ad, word count or dimensions			
Hosted Conference Event bringing 'like minds' together			
Event Sponsorship Could be at different levels based on payment (e.g., Platinum, Gold, Silver)			
Local Event Attendance			

Non-Electronic Marketing Streams	Used in PAST	Use TODAY	Want to use in the FUTURE
(e.g., networking even in a certain niche)			
Service Organization Participation (e.g., volunteering at a soup kitchen or shelter)			
In-Person Social Group Membership (incentivize)			
Holding Special Events Open houses; holiday activities / invites			
Offering Door Prizes (Online or in-person)			
Hard Cover or Softcover Book Publishing (Self-published or through a publisher)			

Monetizing E-Learning Courseware

Non-Electronic Marketing Streams	Used in PAST	Use TODAY	Want to use in the FUTURE
Be the first to follow-up regardless of how			
Remember birthdays and anniversaries			
Distribute Samples			
Visit Prospects			
Re-Visit Prospects			
Travel to NEW Clients			
Tell Stories			
Hold Client Appreciation Events			

Creating Electronic Advertising

NOTE: *This content was taken from and adapted from "How to Create Enterprise-Level Branding for YOUR Business" by Beverly Reynolds; published in 2018; ASIN # B07DL5VS4T.*

Electronic Marketing Streams	Stream Usage Tip
Own or be Interviewed by a Podcast	*If you do not own your own podcast....* When you start your new business, do a search for existing podcast owners and ask to be a guest on their show. Oftentimes these owners will be delighted to have a guest that WANTS to be on their show and can help promote their efforts too. *If you own your own podcast....* Be sure to stay relevant and constant, finding ways to add value while advertising your business.
Marketing to Social Media Followers, Friends or Subscribers	Make sure you have a site for every major social media outlet and that you are posting to these outlets on a regular basis about the benefits you offer to others. This may mean creating free content or free offers to draw attention.
Email Drips or Campaigns (an email list for new product offerings or services)	Purchase a plug-in or find a website hosting service that offers email campaigns or evergreen content as an option. This will give users timely information, such as up-and-coming events, courses or services.
Email Signatures	Use your signature on your business email to advertise your website and offerings. Your signature can be changed as often as you need it to be and is modified in real-time.

Electronic Marketing Streams	Stream Usage Tip
Online Presentations *(animated or static)*	Several social media outlets offer a means for uploading a presentation, such as Microsoft ® PowerPoint ™. This is a good way to offer step-by-step content.
Write or Contribute to Another's Blog	Several website options include a blog or the ability to communicate with users through a blog. Some blogs are paid and some are free. A blog offers you a way to drip scheduled content to your userbase – with or without affiliate links.
Newsletter	If you have a newsletter you create – perhaps based on a template – that is delivered at regular intervals, then clients will see your imagery and message on a regular basis.
Mobile Phone App *(new or modified)*	If you have the technical expertise or the money to have a phone app created, this can be a way to engage your userbase with games, free offers and paid offerings. This format is great for younger, 'techier' users.
Press Releases	Create a press release and give it to the local newspaper – could be for an event or new offering.
eBook	Whether offering a whitepaper or eBook, it is good to offer free content to your visitors – perhaps upon exiting your website. Some people will offer free content in exchange for a name and an email address.

Electronic Marketing Streams	Stream Usage Tip
Live Stream or Webinar	Hold a live event on Facebook or other social media avenues and give a special offer only to attendees at the end.
Whitepaper / Case Study	Whether offering a whitepaper or eBook, it is good to offer free content to your visitors – perhaps upon exiting your website. Some people will offer free content in exchange for an email address.
Website	Be sure to really research the features that your website hosting offers for the monthly or yearly fee. For example, can your blog be hosted in the same place? Does it offer the ability to sell products? Are there fees to sell your products? What payment options are offered? Are there transaction fees? Can you do email drips?
Promotional Video	When you kickoff a new offering or your business itself, it is good to do a promo video for people to connect a face with the new business. This does NOT need to be a 'fancy' or well-edited video.
Free or Paid Social Media Ads	Once you have your business started, it is a good idea to do additional training about how to use social media ads, especially if you are paying a high dollar for the ads.

Electronic Marketing Streams	Stream Usage Tip
Trading Online Ad Space *(with local companies)*	It is a good idea to trade ad space or even offerings with local business owners as a way of creating satisfied clients. Sometimes a testimonial holds far greater value than a monetary sale.

Recreating your Sales Page

- *Think about updating your Sales Page often for ranking* — If you have a Sales Page that advertises your course or FREE webinar, you might want to 'give it a face lift' every now and then. It will not only freshen the look and feel but may make it seem as if it were a brand-new site to web crawler for web ranking.

Utilizing your current Social Media Profiles

Nowadays, it is hard to find a business owner that does not have at least one of the following social media profiles:

- Etsy
- Facebook
- Twitter
- Instagram
- LinkedIn
- Quora

- *Post to your profiles daily* — The list is almost endless and some business owners manage multiples accounts and postings daily.
There are scheduling sites, such as Retortal.com that allow you to schedule most of your social media posts all in one location.

I personally use retortal.com. In fact, if you are interested in Retortal.com, below you will find my distributor link:

http://social.handtdesignmedia.com/signup

- *Consider a social media scheduling service* — If you have a scheduling service, you write the post ahead of time and you can post it to multiple social media channels all at once versus logging into each one individually and copying the post to each on that date.

Designing a FREE Mini-Course

- *Use an LMS and research different marketplaces* — When you purchase a contract or agreement with an LMS, several of these companies have a Marketplace. In the Marketplace, you can often offer a free or discounted course to create interest in the materials and courseware you created.

- *Look for unique ways to create prospects* — The marketplace is a good way to generate prospects as well as current and future sales. If the company you are with does not offer a Marketplace option, search the internet for similar alternatives.

Cross Promotion

- *Promote between your own products* — Once you have a suite of courses, you can cross promote from one course to another. Additionally, in your media avenues, you can also do what is called cross promoting. Cross promoting is where you promote one of your products by using another type of product.

Monetizing E-Learning Courseware

Real Life Application…..

In 2018 I began a blog as a part of my H&T Design Media business. In several blog posts I try to promote my online course material with almost 'shameless plugs.'

That is, I try to promote my own products and services, but also the products and services of others too. Each time I promote someone else's products or services, I am sure to send them a note asking them to 'check out my post.' This creates interactions between myself and other business owners – even if those business owners are my competitors.

Writing Content on Quora.com

- *Answer and ask questions to generate leads online* — Quora.com allows you to be an expert by answering and commenting on posts or questions left by other subscribers. It is FREE to join, but it is a good idea to write a response, add a question or author a blog post on the site daily to be seen and viewed as an expert.

- *Become an expert in your community* — Being an expert has its perks – even if not directly monetary. If you do not get temporarily kicked off the site for promoting your business or offerings or have your posts deleted for violations, you can drive traffic to your site.

- *Traffic is money!* — Adding traffic to your site or blog can mean additional income over time, so it can be worth it if you 'stick with it.'

Running Facebook Ads

- *Marketing does not have to be paid* — You may or may not have the funds to run paid advertisements on Facebook.

If you do, it is a good idea to run targeted ads to specific groups of people versus ads that are spread across an entire geographical area.

Running YouTube Ads

- *Be sure to run targeted ads* — You may or may not have the funds to run paid advertisements on YouTube. If you do, it is a good idea to run targeted ads to specific groups of people versus ads that are spread across an entire geographical area.

- *Consider the type of ads you want to run* — For instance, if you currently monetize your YouTube channel, you will be asked what types of ads you want to run. Pay close attention to this feature once you qualify.

Creating Slide Decks on SlideShare

- *SlideShare allows you to post 'How To' presentations* — Slideshare.com allows you to upload a slide deck from programs like Microsoft® PowerPoint™ or really any program that is similar in nature. These slide decks are viewed by a very large audience that is typically affiliated with LinkedIn.com.

- *LinkedIn is for more than just job seekers – can be for networkers too!* — As you probably already know, LinkedIn.com is seen as a site for job seekers or networkers, so the audience tends to be a bit higher-end than that of Facebook. Job seekers are more times than not older than the average Facebook consumer.

Utilizing Online Groups
(e.g., Facebook Groups, Meetup.com, Eventbrite.com)
Facebook Groups

- *Facebook Groups allow you to connect with like-minded people*

  Facebook groups are a great way to connect with like-minded people outside your traditional personal or business page. That is, a group allows others to post questions, and like Quora.com, you can solve peoples' problems and be viewed as the expert in your field. Just be sure to check the rules and regulations of each group that you join or you could easily get yourself kicked out.

- *Consider starting your own Facebook Group*

  Sometimes for this reason alone, it is a good idea to start your own Facebook group – where you can make or set your own rules and regulations for participants.

Meetup.com

Check social gathering sites for new groups added on a frequent basis.

- *Find people with similar interests*

  For example, Meetup.com is a great way to either join a group or create your own group. Social groups allow you to find people of similar interests and even make new friends.

- *Some groups are fee-based*

  If you are a single parent, nearly every city or metropolitan area contains hundreds and maybe even thousands of social groups for people of a like interest.

If we take our single parent idea, Meetup.com may provide a group to join that is either free, fee-based or allows you to pay by the event this enables YOU to get to know other people or parents that share your same wins and struggles.

- *There is a group for nearly every interest* Meetup events allow people to meet for coffee, partake in family-styled events, compete in a sport or activity, or even, enable people to find new business. To start your own meetup group, there is typically a fee, but that can be recouped if you charge members.

NOTE: *You can encourage membership by offering a trial period and by organizing regular activities. Keeping people engaged is the key.*

Eventbrite.com

Eventbrite is another social site that targets event hosts/goers.

- *You can host or attend a scheduled event* For instance, if you are new to the real estate market, you can look up events in your city dealing with how to write a contract, using market-specific software packages, open houses and other training possibilities.

- *Attach imagery to your event* When you host Eventbrite events, you can even sync your parties and happenings with other social media sites, such as Facebook calendar. This is a good option since it allows images to be attached to attract people at a quick glance.

Be sure that anytime you add a new event (post sign-in), that you not only add imagery, but that you include all the details about the following:

- *Well-researched title*
- *Location details / Address*
- *Detailed description*
- *Date and time of event*
- *Why they should attend*
- *Attention-grabbing statement*
- *Who is invited*
- *Cost of participation*

• *Offer something for FREE as an incentive*	For instance, if I am going to host an essential oils party at the local library, I would want my description to include where and when the event will be held, but also tell them that each guest will receive a <u>FREE</u> gift AND that anyone offering to host the next event at their home or business will receive an additional gift.
• *Grab attention!*	In the above example, you might want to grab attention by telling them that light refreshments or food will be served. Always offer an incentive for people to come to YOUR event over another event happening the same date and time. Attendance incentives might include a free product sample, free usage information (for products), a link to an eBook or even a printed whitepaper or book.

- *Appeal to emotions*

    Another way to capitalize on your audience is to appeal to their emotions. Notice in the previous photo that I added a picture of a dog and a child. People love seeing pictures that portray feelings of some kind.

LAUNCHING YOUR RESULT

Hosting an Open House
You are Invited!

- *Celebrate your achievement*

    You survived the course creation process and now you proudly have a course to launch. It is certainly time to celebrate this lofty achievement. You will want to have an Open House.

- *Choose your event type*

    This could be an informal, open door event by where you announce the new training or educational resources your company is now offering. Make the event at least two hours long and decide the venue well in advance of the scheduled date and time.

- *Send out different types of invites*

    Do not forget to send out both electronic and non-electronic invites. That is, create an event on a site like Eventbrite and send out "snail mail" invites on quality card stock or paper as well.

- *Choose your location wisely*

    You could rent a space, hold the even at your physical business or even open your home. Be sure to have at least light refreshments and drinks.

It is even a good idea to decorate or display a theme that is conducive to your new offerings. The theme should be evident far before the event, including the invites that are send and any postings that are made online.

Having a Course Kick-Off Party

- *Showcase your new course*

  When we use the term kick-off party, we are referring to a project kick-off or customer appreciation event. It is at this event that you will want to showcase your new course, packages or offerings with food and / or drinks. Once again, this event could be held at any location that allows you to get to know the attendees.

- *Turn prospects into repeat clients or customers*

  This is your chance to turn the attendees into prospects or clients. Getting to know each person to the best of your ability is the best way to convert persons to sales. Personal relationships make all the difference.

ABOUT H&T DESIGN MEDIA

H&T Design Media is a social media and branding company. We are an online business focused on helping YOU solve complex marketing and recognizability challenges. You can find us online at *https://www.handtdesignmedia.net*.

ABOUT BEVERLY REYNOLDS

Beverly Reynolds is the owner and a designer for H&T Design Media. She comes to the business with over 20 years of corporate training experience for several Fortune companies. Beverly has created literally hundreds of online courses in several industries, including hospitality, revenue management, oil & gas and death care.

AMAZON BOOKS

Branding your Business: *https://www.amazon.com/Create-Enterprise-Level-Branding-Your-Business/dp/1719475318/ref=sr_1_1?ie=UTF8&qid=1532708285&sr=8-1&keywords=beverly+reynolds+author*

Illustrated Children's Book about Adoption: *https://www.amazon.com/Here-There-Loving-You-Always/dp/194158067X/ref=sr_1_2?ie=UTF8&qid=1532708285&sr=8-2&keywords=beverly+reynolds+author*

Getting the Life of an Instructional Designer: *https://www.amazon.com/Getting-Life-Instructional-Designer-Making/dp/1546429050/ref=sr_1_fkmr0_4?ie=UTF8&qid=1532708285&sr=8-4-fkmr0&keywords=beverly+reynolds+author*

Messaging for your Business – Pocket Edition: *https://www.amazon.com/Messaging-YOUR-Business-Beverly-Reynolds/dp/1721781560/ref=sr_1_fkmr0_2?ie=UTF8&qid=1532708285&sr=8-2-fkmr0&keywords=beverly+reynolds+author*

100 Days of Scrum (Project Management):
https://www.amazon.com/100-Days-Scrum-Iterative-Development-ebook/dp/B0725JQXTF/ref=sr_1_fkmr0_1?ie=UTF8&qid=1532708373&sr=8-1-fkmr0&keywords=beverly+reynolds+author+scrum

Messaging for your Business – Pocket Edition (Kindle E-Book Version): *https://www.amazon.com/Messaging-YOUR-Business-Guide-Consistent-ebook/dp/B07F2YC6JJ/ref=sr_1_fkmr1_3?ie=UTF8&qid=1532708408&sr=8-3-fkmr1&keywords=beverly+reynolds+author+messaging*

ONLINE TRAINING COURSES

Branding Course with nearly 40 timely videos, printable job aids and self-assessments:
https://www.handtdesignmedia.net/p/courses

Additional courses being added soon!

FREE STUFF

FREE webinar on BRANDING YOUR BUSINESS:
https://www.handtdesignmedia.net/pl/31348

FREE blog topics on publishing your book, branding your business and monetizing your course:
https://www.handtdesignmedia.net/blog